TROUBLE FUNK

TROUBLE FUNK

POEMS

Douglas Manuel

Red Hen Press | *Pasadena, CA*

Book design by Mark E. Cull

Library of Congress Cataloging-in-Publication Data

Names: Manuel, Doug, author.
Title: Trouble funk: poems / Douglas Manuel.
Description: First edition. | Pasadena, CA: Red Hen Press, [2022]
Identifiers: LCCN 2022027779 (print) | LCCN 2022027780 (ebook) | ISBN
    9781636280684 (hardcover) | ISBN 9781636280677 (paperback) | ISBN
    9781636280691 (ebook)
Subjects: LCGFT: Poetry.
Classification: LCC PS3613.A5845 T76 2022 (print) | LCC PS3613.A5845
    (ebook) | DDC 811/.6—dc23/eng/20220708
LC record available at https://lccn.loc.gov/2022027779
LC ebook record available at https://lccn.loc.gov/2022027780

Publication of this book has been made possible in part through the generous financial support
of Francesca Bell.

The National Endowment for the Arts, the Los Angeles County Arts Commission, the Ahman-
son Foundation, the Dwight Stuart Youth Fund, the Max Factor Family Foundation, the Pasade-
na Tournament of Roses Foundation, the Pasadena Arts & Culture Commission and the City of
Pasadena Cultural Affairs Division, the City of Los Angeles Department of Cultural Affairs, the
Audrey & Sydney Irmas Charitable Foundation, the Kinder Morgan Foundation, the Meta &
George Rosenberg Foundation, the Albert and Elaine Borchard Foundation, the Adams Family
Foundation, the Riordan Foundation, Amazon Literary Partnership, the Sam Francis Founda-
tion, and the Mara W. Breech Foundation partially support Red Hen Press.

First Edition
Published by Red Hen Press
www.redhen.org

ACKNOWLEDGMENTS

Grateful acknowledgment is made to the editors of the following periodicals and websites where these poems first appeared:

Copper Nickel: "Be My Girl, 1983"; *Indianapolis Review*: "Cosmic Slop, 1969," "Weak at the Knees, 1965"; *Konch Magazine*: "Best of My Love, 1983," "Dazz, 1985," "Get Up to Get Down, 1979," "Make Up Your Mind, 1970," "One Nation Under a Groove, 1974"; *MORIA*: "Fire, 1975," "Flashlight, 1981," "Slippin' into Darkness, 1969"; *New Orleans Review*: "Are You Single?, 1981"; *Pleiades*: "Go for Your Guns, 1977"; *Pratik*: "Do You Wanna Go Party, 1980," "Fun, 1979," "Let's Get Small, 1986," "Mothership Connection, 1975"; and *ZYZZYVA*: "Humpin', 1980," "Mustang Sally, 1964."

for Uncle Jamie, aka Jamming Jamie Coles

And for Dad, aka Jose the DJ, aka Big Jack, aka King Flex,
aka the King of Locust Street

CONTENTS

I

Let's Get Small, 1986   17

Go For Your Guns, 1977   19

Humpin', 1980   20

Get Up To Get Down, 1979   21

Mothership Connection, 1975   22

Are You Single?, 1981   24

Make Up Your Mind, 1970   26

Our Love, 1972   28

These Eyes, 1986   29

Fire, 1975   30

Happy Feelings, 1970   32

Your Love (Means Everything To Me), 1981   34

Be My Girl, 1983   36

Cosmic Slop, 1969   38

Knock On Wood, 1974   39

One Of A Kind (Love Affair), 1985   40

Miss You, 1979   41

Outside Woman, 1979   42

I Like It, 1985   43

Flirt, 1970   44

Back In Love, 1982   46

Do You Wanna Go Party, 1980   47

Traffic Jammer, 1973   48

Shakey Ground, 1978   49

Got To Be Enough, 1982   50

Anticipation, 1986   52

II

Toast To The Fool, 1983   55

Stop, Look, Listen (To Your Heart), 1973   56

Let's Straighten It Out, 1980   58

Flashlight, 1981   59

One Chain Don't Make No Prison, 1979   60

She Works Hard For The Money, 1984   61

Best Of My Love, 1983   62

Slippin' Into Darkness, 1969   64

Fun, 1979   65

One Nation Under A Groove, 1974   66

Stay In My Corner, 1977   67

Memory Lane, 1985   68

What Do The Lonely Do At Christmas, 1986   69

Red Hot Momma, 1967   70

Do You Love What You Feel, 1974   72

Dream Merchant, 1985   73

I Ain't Gonna Stand For It Anymore, 1981   74

I Can Make You Dance, 1983   76

Weak At The Knees, 1965   78

Dazz, 1985   80

I Wish It Would Rain, 1977   82

Got To Love Somebody, 1987   83

Mustang Sally, 1964   84

Time Will Reveal, 1987   86

TROUBLE FUNK

Each of the poems in this collection is titled after a song. These songs are a soundtrack for this book. If it's possible and accessible for you, please listen to each of these songs in the order provided here after, while, and/or before you read this book. My father loved to play all of these songs when he was a DJ in the late 70s and early 80s. The dates next to each title indicate when the narrative action of the poem takes place.

I

LET'S GET SMALL, 1986

Same scream since the night before—
she locks herself in the bathroom.
He holds up the bathroom door with his back.

Today's her birthday.

Another job gone, the song
of another woman all over his lips. Caught,
she could taste it.

She screams. He screams. They scream.
They scream. He screams. She screams.
She screams. He screams. Their scream

the same scream they began with, the same
scream will end them. But, really,
it's older than that, deeper than that, and oh so Black.

The same scream since Middle Passage,
since slavery,
since Reconstruction,
since Jim Crow,
since Great Migration,
since redlining,
since Civil Rights.

So many screams slicing love.

Music, the stitches. Forgiveness inside a drum.

He walks to the record player, puts on their song.
The time's 4/4, hard on the downbeats, staccato—
something to dance to,
something to survive through,
something to die to.

The bathroom door sighs open,
a mouth full of silence.

GO FOR YOUR GUNS, 1977

Year of the *Roots* miniseries. They peep how
Kunta won't be Toby, how he pretends

he won't need that foot, how he ain't afraid to lose
it. When Damon ain't here at Denise's house,

he stays in his van, his own mobile home—always
nowhere to go, no real home since his stepdaddy told

him to go again. *I'm gonna paint the van green*, he tells her.
Emerald or jade, something—.

Regal or royal, she interrupts, placing two fingers on his lips
to shush him and smooth his mustache. Above their heads,

adorning the wall, a velvet painting of a Black woman
birthing the universe from her skull, afro aglow with thoughts,

galaxies ripe with rings circling planets, beltways of stars lit
as if they were paths leading to all the great nowheres

they could never be. *You know, you ain't gotta leave. You ain't
gotta live in that raggedly van*, she says. *Lighters, records,*

cords, pipes, razors everywhere. Her living room all dark
except for the glow from the TV illuminating the line

from slavery to their very bodies, still Black, still not free, always
needing to think on their feet, always needing to be ready to flee.

HUMPIN', 1980

The crowd wildin' out, lost and caught
    in the snare of the beat, in harmony,
        more like one body, not many—Damon's

the brain running thangs. *1-2-3-4,*
    leave your worries at the door. 5-6-7-8,
        you better make your booty shake.

His crown beads of sweat, not thorns,
    more precious than diamonds. *Work it,*
        baby, work it, baby, work it. The dance

floor more sanctuary than club, and he's
    the priest. When he was an altar
        boy, his back was always to the crowd.

Not now. Now the strobe lights are
    the whitest thing in the room, and the groove
        is the only god anyone is praying to.

Denise has never loved him more
    than when he's commanding the dance
        floor, but now perceives him as she has never

before: a man cloaked with that much glory,
    surrounded by so many, soaring with that
        much power, can only end up alone

and back down on the floor.

GET UP TO GET DOWN, 1979

Denise can't find herself, can't see herself, only Damon—
always only Damon. She stands behind him in the mirror,

adjusting his tie from behind, asking him, *Does it look good,
does it feel fine, does it feel too tight?* The way his lips reveal

his brash half-smile answers her questions. When she isn't
working at Guide Lamp, most of Denise's life's spent

taking care of Damon: ironing those cut-your-finger-sharp
creases in his slacks, scrubbing his shirt collars with bleach

until those yellowed sweat-spots release themselves
from the fabric, cooking the meals he devours without

even leaving her a little bit for her own plate. He's always
on the go, fleeing, in the act of leaving: *I gotta go see*

*about twenty dollars I let Odelle hold I gotta go set up
for tonight's set I gotta go play pool I gotta go play dominos*

*I gotta go throw dice with Jamie and them I gotta go
to the record store in Indy for some new music.* The same old

excuses descend from his mouth as routinely as December snow.
It's all the same, all the same. He always has some good reason

for leaving her home all alone, all night long, staying up
until she curses herself out in the mirror, still

unable to find herself there, still invisible to herself and everyone else.

MOTHERSHIP CONNECTION, 1975

Before DJ-scratch, the breakdown was all drum-fill,
handclap, bass-slap, guitar-wail. Talk over the track, not yet
rap yet rap always.

Is funk. Is rock. Is blues. Is jazz. Is ragtime. Is work

song. In short: is Black, always Black on both sides all the way down.

Black on Black on Black on Black.

Same scream since—.

He rests acid on her tongue.

You sure it's okay, she asks. Lies sleep
on the tip of his tongue. Always and forever.

Don't wake them. She must never.

Bellbottoms crowning platform shoes.
The groove moves Denise and Damon, dons the crown, is god.

Late afternoon turns the evening moonlit, turns
to bedroom, turns to them in the dawn, wet from sweat,
the same bed, the same breath.

Each body on its own riff.

Pawns of acid-trip, of music,
of forget for the first time but not the last.

A whole summer they tumblel through a sonic-drug-buzz.
He spins. She assembly-lines, a Midwest song, a story

of factories and dancehalls. *We're hiring*, she says,
if you ever want a real job.

ARE YOU SINGLE?, 1981

for the family of Michael Donald

Released and returned, the hostages invades
        each and every news segment. The new president,

a former actor (Damon told her—Denise had never
        heard of *The Killers* or *Law and Order*) speaks

with a sparkle that mirrored the glinting glow
        ricocheting off Damon's juicy, soaking wet Jheri curl.

Denise's matched—his and her Jheri curls.
        Tonight would be theirs, no

dance hall, no women surrounding the turntables,
        no waiting for him to finish working

the room, no prying eyes calling to question
        all of her fashion choices. Tonight would be a fancy

dinner, somewhere Black folks don't normally go,
        somewhere she ain't been before. She outlines

her lips, fills them, smacks them—she's almost
        tempted to kiss the glass, almost tempted to love herself.

Giving her hair one more pat, she's set, strolls out
        in her ankle-hose, searching for her flats. In front

of the TV, she only sees his back: it's slightly atremble.
        When she gets closer, she can see the tears.

What's wrong? she asks. *They just left him swinging there,*

he says. *Who, who, who, who*, she asks, thinking
        it was his brother, his uncle, one of his hardheaded

cousins. Then, the anchor announces his name plain
        and a matter-of-fact-like just as he would warn

of rain or an overcast day, *Michael Donald,*
        son of Beulah Mae and David Donald, lynched.

MAKE UP YOUR MIND, 1970

Girl, you can't be down on the floor
on all fours, Denise's mama says.
Your knees and elbows will get too dark
and won't a nare man want you when

you get grown. Denise doesn't wanna get
grown. She's heard Nella and Lisa talking
about acting grown and playing *Lay and Stay*
with Floyd and Marcus. Denise still wants

to play Tonk, Pokeno, or Spades with her
Auntie Daisy, who knows everything
about basketball, gutting fish, and music.
Playing *Lay and Stay* ain't on Denise's mind.

Saturday morning, when the grass's still
wet from whatever sweats and labors
in the night, and the moon's in the opposite
side of the sky as the sun, Denise sprints

the full three blocks to her auntie's house.
Smoking Pall Mall Red 100's, Auntie Daisy,
gorgeous as day, perches on the porch with Denise's cards,
waiting for her. Denise asks her auntie

exactly what playing *Lay and Stay* is.
Daisy replies, *Girl, come sit down here*
and play these cards. We always playing
cards, ya hear me now, always playing cards.

Everything a card game. Denise plops down
and eyes her cards. *What you bidding, Baby?*
Denise answers, *I ain't got nothing. I gotta go
board with four,* her knitted brow looking over

the cards. Daisy sucks her teeth, shakes her
head, *Tsk, tsk, no risk gets you nowhere
and nothing forever. I'mma put you down
for five, and you better play like it is your life.*

OUR LOVE, 1972

Before the dancehalls, before
the rec-center parties, before his
turntables turned all of Anderson
out, before Damon's name was
in everyone's mouth, the best place
on planet earth, the best place
to make your body shake, pop,
and work, was the Roller Rink. Hex-
boogie shuffle, dip, drop, and spin,
the world only them, the music
a religion, but this ain't no church.
Denise's in the corner of the arcade—
Damon's trying put his hands up
her skirt. A quick elbow and a smile
that's more menacing than flirting
and she's back skating circles,
her body back in the beat. Her girls
find her. They all know the song,
the way to dance, to strike then flee.
Look at them jamming, they almost
look like one single grooving body.

THESE EYES, 1986

Damon thought it could only happen to gay people,
but the *Herald Bulletin* said it clear, cold, plain:

Kokomo Boy HIV Positive.

The little boy wasn't nothing
but 13, which was the same name as the freeway

that would take you from Kokomo to Anderson.
Due north on the 13 and west on the 35,

and you'll be there before three good songs
played on the radio. In Kokomo, in 1930,
they lynched a man, Damon's mama told him:

all the white folks in Kokomo came out to see that

brother dangle from the tree. When Damon was 13,
in history class, he learned that Kokomo was named
after Chief Kokomoko.

                    The class laughed
as the teacher told them that *Ma-Ko-Ko-Mo*
was the name of the chief's tribe.

FIRE, 1975

A must, a nickname, something one needed,
as if birth names weren't enough:

Sugarfoot, Ls, Junebug, Hog, Bottom-rung,
Words, Fox, and Doc Bird.

                    Names he's heard,
names of other DJs, names nicked from quick

thoughts and pinprick needle tongues. He needed one.
How to find one? Earn it, search for it, make it,

rake the leafy lawn of his mind to see what
he will find.

                 No reds, oranges, and yellows
swirling anymore. Now all is winter; all is

the muted snow blunting the bladed edges
of the world. Him and her in the tight curl

of love, cuddling, hard to tell him from her,
her from him.

                How 'bout DJ Damon? he begins,
slicing the silence with the heat of his breath.

Her left hand combs through the hairs of his chest.
Don't you wanna be more than you? she asks.

Outside, the wind whets the cold, icicles
sleek out to daggers hanging from the awning.

How can I be more than me?
                              he says. She

giggles. *Stick with me,*
                    and you'll see. You'll see.

HAPPY FEELINGS, 1970

The songs were more
sad than happy,
the church was more
white than Black. Part
of her thought her
family liked that.

Them the only Blacks

in the pews. The priest
lipping Latin. The whole
experience about the body
in motion: Sit in
the back, stand up, head
down, sing. Sing. Sing.
Sit down. Head down.
Know your place. Never
forget your place.

Stand up. Sing. Sit down.

Pray. Pray. Sing. Hold
hands. Sit down. Kneel.
Kneel. Know your place.
Never forget your place.
Kneel. Kneel. Eat cracker.
Sip wine. Pray. Kneel.

Pray. Pray hard. Pray harder.
This won't last much longer.
Know your place.
Never forget your place.

Still, she'll be Blacker
than the devil's heel when
they all step out into the white world.

YOUR LOVE (MEANS EVERYTHING TO ME), 1981

Damon doesn't remember
how old he was when
he saw his grandpa on the ground
hogtied, the police laughing.

This will teach ya, they said. Damon

doesn't remember learning
about the Klan, but he remembers
the stories of crosses cutting
the night open with their flames.

He's seen the charred grass, black
as the pupil of an eye. The first time

he was called *Nigger*, he remembers.

The word hurt more than Tommy's
fist colliding with Damon's lips
for asking Amy, Tommy's sister, to be
his Valentine. Sucking

his bottom lip and swallowing blood,
Damon's anger sizzled the whole
way to the principal's office. Whipped
at school and once he got home:

Damon's mama made him get a switch.

This will teach ya, she said. The last
time Damon talked smart
to the cops, the barrel of the gun
was warm against his face

as if the cop had just shot somebody.

This will teach ya.

BE MY GIRL, 1983

For her, a day off from work

was manna to the tongue.

The best part of the song

looped to play again

and again as Damon learns

how to make it do what it do.

A day off from work was the sky

releasing a load of rain

from its shoulders,

the river finding the ocean

after no-sight-sliding

down mountainsides

and eating soil to make wet,

black riverbeds. A day off

from work was a day without

any voice but the one in her head

to keep her company. She got

to play any song she pleased.

COSMIC SLOP, 1969

All Damon ever wanted was a gold watch
to match the gold chain he found hanging
from the gaunt arm of a mulberry tree

by the White River. As if left there
just for him, an omen
from the Lord, something to tell him

what was in store for him beyond the forest
floor he kept his eyes on as he trudged
the uneven path back to Raible Ave.

All he ever wanted was not to be
so fat, for the girls to talk to him
even when they didn't need help

with their math, for the skinny boys not to pull
down his pants and sprint away as they laughed.
An ace pilot like those brothers from Tuskegee,

that's what he wanted to be. A chest full of medals
and the respect of all of Anderson.
All he ever wanted to be

was a name that never slipped a tongue,
one that was never forgotten but repeated
again and again like the best part of a song, the refrain.

KNOCK ON WOOD, 1974

The jumper was red, white, and blue.
Not that anyone would notice,
her red robe reached down to her feet.
But the jumper was indeed red
white, and blue. She saw it, clear
as a day on its way into being morning.
With honors is how she graduated—
the degree says it. She says it
to herself. Why doesn't anyone else
say it? *With honors. Denise graduated*
with honors, she says it aloud.
She says it loud. Say it aloud. Say it
aloud. Say it loud! Why doesn't anyone
say it? Why doesn't she walk out of this house
and drive her car out of Anderson, out
of Indiana, out, out, out? Strolling across
the stage was easy. Everybody
was clean, in their best and clapping. Why
ain't leaving as easy as screaming?

ONE OF A KIND (LOVE AFFAIR), 1985

The crucifix in the center of her chest,
Christ in the center of her life, she likes
what that feels like, something stable

to hang on to, somebody who'll listen,
who won't judge. Power centered
by her heart. She leans back into

the chair, let out a laugh, a laugh freer
than the mouth of the Mississippi
finding the gulf, freer than dandelion

seeds caught in the breeze's breath,
freer than a whisper turning to a yell, than
hair brushed out from rollers. Putting

her feet up on the ottoman, she crosses
them and then herself. Rosary beads
move before her fingers do. Prayers

lift and flit, lift and flit, just as the smoke
will later than evening, when the music
plays drums with God's head.

MISS YOU, 1979

The gas line hooks and crooks
     its way back from Locust St.
to the Avenue. In the jade van
     Damon's all sweat, drips trickling
and tickling down his back, his shirt
     refusing to let him go. Not much
unlike the way Tina didn't want
     him to leave this morning. *You know,*
he told her, *Denise ain't riding*
     with that. He's uncomfortable.
The heat's too much for the cigarette
     dangling out from the side
of his mouth. Tina shifted her weight
     from one foot to the other before
lifting herself onto her toes and kissing
     him right in the center of his brow
where Denise always says his third eye
     resides. With a quick flick of the wrist,
he swipes away his sweat. Sighing, he replays
     the night before. Denise's
Nova zooms by on Locust St.
     She doesn't even wave. *How could she*
not see me? Couldn't she see me?

OUTSIDE WOMAN, 1979

A white Chrysler New Yorker,
      the hood wide as a mountain's backside.
She paid for it with cash. *You ought*

      to have seen the salesman's face, Damon.
            You ought to have seen it. Denise laughs,
      head back. Her white scarf's too tight.

She loosens it, takes it off, stands.
      Damon's already dancing over
to the record player. He has the perfect

      song. The song is perfect because he plays
            it for her, plays it right then, shines
      a light on her. A perfect song to shake,

drop, and rock to. On the front porch,
      her chair is rusted yellow, his silver.
They pass a cigarette. They pass a pint,

      a joint, another pint, a cigarette. *Do you*
            want to lie on it? Damon answers
      with a nod and they're off in a trot

to the New Yorker. Head to head,
      they sprawl across the hood. *Turn it on,*
she says, *so it's warm and ready.*

I LIKE IT, 1985

After Damon got out of jail the first time,
Denise attacked him with love, threw her
arms around him, just kept saying, *Sorry,*
Baby. Sorry, Baby, I didn't get you sooner.

After Damon got out of jail the second time,
Denise smacked him when they got in the car.
This shit again, Damon, were her only words.
The radio, windshield wipers, angered whispers.

After Damon got out of jail the third time,
Denise about didn't come get him. Her temper
the color of fire. Damon on the same shit.
The same shit song from the same shit liar.

After Damon got out of jail the fourth time,
Denise hadn't had her monthly in months. Winter
was the season. A little swelling in her ankles
and feet. She dare not tell Damon, the coward.

After Denise got Damon out of jail for the last time,
she dropped him off by his mama's, on the corner
of Locust and Arrow. Teddy was standing there
high as pinetree tops, sipping a pint of Thunderbird.

FLIRT, 1970

After his stepdaddy lost the family
store, before he was a DJ controlling
the dance floor, after he shot up
to 6'4", before he met Denise,
his forever lover, his amore, Damon
washed cars for living. It was better
than cutting grass, trimming edges,
and shearing bushes, better than
scouring through trash cans early
in the morning for scrap metal,
copper, and cans, better than selling
bootlegged liquor, reefer, acid,
or coke, better than riding the bench
on some football field or basketball
court—Damon couldn't play
no sports—better than watching
his mama tread the currents of her
liquor bottles, better than gambling
after school, fingering the eyes
of some dice or knocking the cue ball
playing pool, better than chasing girls
around the skating rink only to hear
their refusals and laughter sink
into his chest. The way they called
him fat he'd never forget. Yes,
washing cars was the best idea,
spotting dirt and with simple working
circles scrubbing it until it disappeared.
This fast gratification—the way

he, fatherless, fat-boy Damon
could instantly affect the world—
the first drug he got high on, the first
of his many insatiable satisfactions.

BACK IN LOVE, 1982

She knew she wasn't alone. Denise
could call Jasmine, Lonnie, Pam,

any of them would answer and then
they'd all be there. They'd be going

somewhere, getting bottle service,
the chill of the ice bucket cool enough

for her to lay her head next to when
she's too gone, too many sips, too

much dancing. She can't see beyond
the length of her nose. Giggles, giggles.

Girl, you gonna be all right? Pam
asks. Denise has never been better

at being worse. The red ice bucket
is the same red Pam is wearing. Pam
went to the Army but don't ever
talk about her tours. Pam wipes Denise's

hair from her face, hands her water.
The bassline in her ears, in her chest,

beating her heart, the liquor stirring
her anger, Denise stands and is off

to the rhythm, to the dance floor again.

DO YOU WANNA GO PARTY, 1980

She asks if she's something to come home to,

if music is all, if he's on a pedestal
from which he could only fall, if having

the world in your palm means anything at all
if you drop it. She's looking in
the mirror. She sees him, sees him more
than herself. Outside, below zero, and all the potholes

are full of frozen snow, the type that might
make him slip tonight. She told him to wear

boots instead of dress shoes, handed him his pistol.
Him and his blowout-afro-dreams, her the seams
holding their sweater together. Cold, their words.
Tears, their tradition. She keeps time by the sound
of his feet, sleeps when he wakes, works
when he sleeps. The night is a siren. He wants
the song to last all night long, wants their life
to spin the circles of rhythm, the beat
of repeat, his solo the whole show.

TRAFFIC JAMMER, 1973

Nobody really knows how, but everybody really knows
how it all started—the way history's more, not less,
told from the tip-top of the tongue. Meaning it's a lie,
meaning that it's true to you, you, you, but not me,
me, me. Denise isn't crazy. The white boy slapped her
booty. The newspaper has some of the truth, too: it was
a cake-cutter afro pick that Damon hit that white boy
with. Then, fists, more fists, kicks, knives, and blood.
A school closed for a week. Handcuffs, you know
who wore them: Damon and his friends, all of them,
none of the white boys, none of the teachers who cast
their eyes aside as white fists found Black faces,
as baseball bats and balls, as chemistry beakers, flasks
and test tubes became weapons, as locker doors slammed
shut on Black skulls. Outnumbered as usual, behind
enemy lines as usual, stacked in the back of cop cars
as usual—but no silent swinging bodies this time.

SHAKEY GROUND, 1978

When Kojak got back
from prison, Damon was 15,

When Kojak gave Damon
a little deuce-deuce, he was 16.

When Kojak first let Damon
hold some money, he was 18.

When Kojak made the girl do
what she did, Damon smiled,

laughed as he pulled up his pants.
He was 20. When Kojak took

him on his first lick, the pistol
shook in his hand. Dandelions

blowing off the stem is what
he thought about. He was 22.

When Kojak got shot, their eyes
locked and then Kojak fell

and kept falling, falling,
bleeding, bleeding, no matter

how hard Damon tried he couldn't
stop it, the blood, the fall.

GOT TO BE ENOUGH, 1982

If she could, Denise would weave
all the lessons each of them taught
her into her hair so that she could
keep it there forever and have
all that wisdom with her always, right
close to her mind so that every time
trouble showed its ugly behind she'd
be ready for it.
                    Aunt Daisy's skin
was closer to gold than yellow
and was dark all around the knees
and elbows. She could gut a fish
with a cigarette still lit and hanging
from the side of her mouth. Card games
were her job: Denise never knew her to go
to no work.
                    Denise's mama's skin was more
like charcoal and, boy, did the woman
smolder and stay lit forever once
she got burning. Curses fell from her
tongue, and she carried a pistol
in her purse. She kept a job: doing hair,
cleaning houses, cleaning chitterlings,
watching babies. Granny drank shine.

Granny's mama didn't have to pick
no cotton because Papa picked so much.
Granny would let flies stay on her,
without a movement, would
just keep telling her story
as if nothing was on her. Granny said,

A man ain't good for nothing
except his dick and his dollars.

ANTICIPATION, 1986

Sometimes the lights would shine just right,

wrap them up all tight as they slow-grooved, the beat

ingrained in the sway of their hips—release

from the workday week, from never being good

enough, passed over, overlooked, left out, from

the mounting glaring that rode you from the time you left

the house until the door closed behind you to announce

you home. Love can rise like bread from a spinning track.

Music can give back everything you lack. Only

problem is it won't stay like that. It just won't

stay. Oh to be the record left on, spinning,

instead of the ceased song.

II

TOAST TO THE FOOL, 1983

They kissed as if the other's mouth
was the cure for a disease they both
carried for so long they forgot they had it.
A disease no doctors could spot, a sickness
that was beyond the eyes of their cousins,
aunties, uncles, their grandmas,
their grandpas, their mamas, their—

they both didn't have no daddies.

They kissed as if the kiss was the last
thing they would do with their lives,
as if the horns of The End were loud
in their ears, the ground was shifting
below them about to take them forever
under. They both could always see the end
of things, the lastness of last always on—

a dead daddy is a long, long, song.

They kissed as if they were free, as if
the color of their skin didn't scar a target
around their bodies, as if the law couldn't
make them crawl, the police with their
guns drawn, their bodies were sacred
and safe instead of scarce and sacrilegious.
They kissed. They kissed. They kissed
as if music saves, as if loves saves,
because it does. Let's hope it does. It does.

It doesn't.

STOP, LOOK, LISTEN (TO YOUR HEART), 1973

Denise had always heard talk of wars:

The Korean War:

> why Uncle Cecil don't walk
> good and can feel the rain coming, why
> he hears voices only the dog hears, why he peers
> into the black evening sky, why he burned
> his whole house down
> with a cigarette.

> The Vietnam War: why

almost everybody she know know
somebody who ain't come back. Her senior
year, there were so many funerals. TV

showed flag-draped caskets. Denise knew
Bobby didn't need to get high all the time
until he came back from Vietnam.

> The war on drugs:

somebody said something about it at work, when
they were clocking in, somebody said, *Nixon
wasn't playing no games.* Denise didn't think

of Damon and what he was slanging, didn't
think of what Titi was, what Deon was, what
JT was, what almost everyone she knew was doing.

Well, she did, but not for too long—there used to be

a war on poverty

and that didn't last that long.

LET'S STRAIGHTEN IT OUT, 1980

On her lap, bouncing back and forth,
he's in an olive and gold little leisure suit.
Damon's mama kept him sharp now.

She would tell him, *You never know*
who you going to see. It's a photo he keeps
in his wallet: him a bouncing baby

boy, his mama's smile framed
by curtain bangs, a bit forced.
Denise wonders if he can see that

as she puts the photo back in
his wallet and then tosses
his jeans into the washer.

FLASHLIGHT, 1981

The Avenue: Lee's Pool Hall, The Mirage, The Red Spot, Sonny Ray's,

the smell of beers, brown liquor, and all the fears
of people who consult the edge every day. There is he.
There he always is. Amidst risk, behind the shell of a building left to die,
poor, gutted-open, and Black, Damon's a grace note
in the melody of a dice game: fate and faith stone-threw,
money moving so quickly no one owns it. Guns. Blades,
razor and switch. Back Do' Lil' Joe, The Hard Way, Up Pops the Devil,
and the black glassy eyes of snakes. He just got done
spinning, got money to spend, money to lend, money
to pretend that this him is the real him, the best him. He's losing
less than he wins. Walking home alone heavier, he eyes a pigeon.
No, it's a crow. From the shadows, it rises with a matchstick
in its mouth. *Some hardhead put a pistol on the nape of my neck,*

he tells her later at her house, shows her, touches that soft spot. *It was cold.*

ONE CHAIN DON'T MAKE NO PRISON, 1979

At the Rio, a chocolate brown wicker chair
met your gaze right as you stepped in
the door. The way it stood out against
the fading red paint of the club's wall

      would draw your eye right there,
      and that's where couples took Polaroids.
      Denise sat on his lap. Their suits match:
      gray slacks, blazers black, and gray

apple hats. *Couldn't tell them nothing,*
is what everybody would say. One hand
on hers. She's not reaching back. One
hand on his drink and he's about to put

      another back. They look so good, both
      of them in their shades, looking out,
      showing out, hoping everybody can spot
      them without really ever seeing them.

SHE WORKS HARD FOR THE MONEY, 1984

The lightest turquoise dresses,
hats of the same hue, gloves

white as doves against their chocolate
skins. A summer wedding. Lonnie

was the first to get hitched. Denise
told her not to, Pam told her not to,

Jasmine told her, Lonnie's own mama
told her Greg wasn't worth a damn.

Greg was always gambling with Damon.
Denise didn't like explaining

the differences between Damon and Greg
to her friends, but to her they were clear

and apparent. Damon was the best
DJ to ever live. Damon was—. Damon was

her man, the man she fell in love with,
and she wasn't no fool. She ain't

never been no fool. She been a lotta
things but never that, never that.

Denise's hat flew off when she tried
to catch Lonnie's bouquet: white roses,

baby's breath, the thinnest turquoise
ribbon just holding everything together.

BEST OF MY LOVE, 1983

To hate Damon would be easier if she didn't

hit him first. Her grandma always said, *If you*
bold enough to throw one, you better be bold
enough to catch one. Denise didn't give a damn.

When he came home with lipstick on his collar
she hit him like she was a man. She wasn't no
step-out-on-me, sleep-alone-all-night-type

of woman. To hate him would be easier if she did
what her mama told her and always did what he said,
if she listened with the love's shine in her eyes

whenever he spoke, if she swallowed all her dreams
without choking, only throating the staccato,
vibrato notes of his musical ambitions. To hate him

would be easier if he didn't watch basketball
with her grandma, granny with her snuff, him
with his bootlegged liquor from his cousin and them.

Denise could hate him, could kick him out, could
leave him for good if he hadn't whooped
that white boy who smacked her ass, if she hadn't

kissed Charles when Damon was gone spinning
in Indy. Now, if she could somehow look him dead
in the eye without seeing that chubby boy

snot-nose-crying under a mulberry tree after
his daddy died, she'd leave. It would be easy
to hate him, easy to rip her life apart, easy to

stitch it, herself, back together, to make a new start.

SLIPPIN' INTO DARKNESS, 1969

MORE SOUL was what the sign said—well, used to say, before
gusts, cold, rain, snow, and no money made the R fade away.

Now the butterfly collars and halter tops call it *Mo Soul*
and wanna know who Mo is. *Ain't no Mo here,* he always

tells them as he takes their orders. *Let me get the Dark
Meat Two-Piece Special.* His afro trying to escape the confines

of his hairnet, his forehead lined with acne, sweat beads,
and chicken grease. This evening, him and his mama

run the whole place. His stepdaddy gone to The Avenue;
his real daddy got shot on The Avenue, his uncle too, trying to

make right what happened that night. *Damon, boy, you know
yo' mama be putting her whole foot in those greens.* Etta Mae,

from the kitchen, say, *You just want some of this honey,
Junebug. Ain't nobody studyin' you.* If his stepdaddy was here,

he'd be upside her head, and Junebug would have a mouthful
of gun shaft choking his throat. If his stepdaddy was here,

they wouldn't be closing early; they wouldn't be dancing,
mother and son doing the Funky Chicken and the Bump,

wishing The Avenue would make her a widow again.

FUN, 1979

A reason, no, a need to speak low-ended. Season
    runs up on Lent. Ashes, ashes, her fists knock
        him down. Now, her body lifts, then minor scale,

next, not free but caged in his arms. Muted-bass-
    slap. Their history, their beings overflowing
        with needs unmet: threat, threat, threat, that's the color,
the sweat, the anger that seeps, then freezes. Snow's hour
    of without. Make him sip winter. Make him
        tongue cold light poles. The streets always calling.

She's a brewed-cold evening, him all want and plead,
    all powerful, all deceiving. *Coward. You little coward!*
        His pants still hold the creases from the starch.

Ironing done by her. *I didn't lie*, he promises. He always
    promises. Promises, promises, they're all over
        the ground. Promises and her teeth, she picks them up.

ONE NATION UNDER A GROOVE, 1974

Damon doesn't know who his real daddy is,
only met him once. He gave Damon
a flattened penny with a hole right in the middle
of Lincoln's head and told Damon he could make
a necklace out of it. Damon lost it but remembers
having it, the same way he remembers
that bruise on his arm from when he tried
to catch the switch midair. His mama's tears,
his stepdaddy's fury, Damon remembers.
His stepdaddy lost the family store, lost himself
to alcohol and pain pills. If he could, Damon would
never say his stepdaddy's name aloud. Damon high
all the time on weed, speed, smiling tabs torn
from a sheet, he tried best as he could
to quell the need not to be dead
like his real daddy. A shotgun shell burst
his forehead open like a dropped watermelon. At least
that's what Uncle Trevor and them said.

STAY IN MY CORNER, 1977

In Denise's eyes the only
holiday better than Christmas
is the Fourth of July. Burning
charcoal, the smell's been filling
the house since can't-see-
in-the-morning. This day's
one of the only days Damon
finds his way out of bed
before day. Denise shucks corn,
stuck in reverie. A melody,
lifts from her lips, one you
wouldn't notice her humming
if you weren't close
enough. Damon busts in,
cracks her dream, carrying
his latest batch: racks
of ribs, some spicy brats.
Even when he doing right,
he does her wrong. A kiss,
a quick slap on her backside
and he's back outside, distant
and gone to that not-here-but-here
place he always hides.

MEMORY LANE, 1985

Ain't no telling how it would start:

Damon's eyes would sharpen, following
her, almost clawing after her. Her body
brought to nervous perspiration
from his glance. The feeling of stumbling
unknowingly into a stiff left hook blazes her still.
The feeling of breath snatched from lungs,
knees buckling. Denise knows the taste
of blood in her mouth.

She's eaten his fist and asked for more.

Denise knows the sound of everything
they never talk about, the silence his apologies
slice open, how he sits back, crosses his legs,
and clears his throat before he's quiet again.
Not talking is his power. Screaming
quietly is his power. The size of his body,
his power. Her power? Her body and how she can
deny him the pleasure of it, playing keep-away
to placate him while raking these words across his face,
You ain't shit and ain't ever gonna be shit.

His desire, his pride, those soft spots can stop him.

WHAT DO THE LONELY DO AT CHRISTMAS, 1986

At first it was just a rumor—something
far away and invisible but on the way,
like the hand of God, his wrath, retribution,

justice. At first it seemed like a good idea,
a way to make the party never stop, a way
to keep dancing, to keep the song going,

the record spinning, the money coming in.
The money got so big so fast. There was
so much money so fast. It couldn't, wouldn't

last. At first it was so very fun, but then
there were guns. The guns got so big, so fast.
There were so many guns, and the guns

brought blood. The blood. The blood. The blood.
There was so much blood. The blood spread
so fast. The bodies. The bodies. He wasn't addicted.

At first it was just one rock. It was just one rock.

RED HOT MOMMA, 1967

*Have you been your other self
today?* Auntie Daisy asks, her eyes

loom over her cards. They are
playing Tonk. *I ain't got nothing*

that match, Denise replies, not
answering. *Your other self*

been you today? Auntie Daisy tries
the question a different way.

I'm always me and the other me,
Denise throws down a spread,

Ten of Clubs, Jack, Queen.
Nothing that match my ass,

Auntie Daisy says between laughs
as she puts her cards down to light

a cigarette. Their birthdays are
the same day, June 11, Geminis—

minds twined, changeable
as the whims of the wind, their

thoughts airy as the smoke
bending itself around Auntie Daisy's

face. *I know what you mean*, says
Auntie Daisy as she leans her head

aslant. *I'm always both mes too: one
on her knees, praying and crying,*

*one cussing her out, telling her,
"Enough is enough, get up, girl, get up."*

DO YOU LOVE WHAT YOU FEEL, 1974

Before everybody came out
to the club to get lost, to forget
loss, to get free, to spend their money,
to spend their sweat, to spin
their very bodies in the sound
of Damon's song selection, on Friday
evenings, the Wigwam, the second biggest
basketball gym in the whole country,
was the best place to be in Anderson.
The best part for Damon was Denise
with him, on his arm, making him
a star, more famous than Kojak,
more famous than Petey who
would score 24 points that very night,
more famous than Jackie Flint,
the white man coaching the almost
all Black team to victory. Timmy Green,
Chad Hill, Colin Grant, and Josh
Kemp, only there to be white,
to shoot 3s and keep the booster club
happy, the money coming in, the country
club crowd smiling in stands, cheering
for an "Indian" mascot, dressed in what
they thought natives wore, loving Black
folks only if they score, winning the game
for white folks. Encore. Encore. Encore!

DREAM MERCHANT, 1985

The years stood
          right in front

of her face, all
          she saw. Mornings,

their faces in
          the same mirror,

sharing the same
          sink, their toothbrushes

in the same cup,
          the foamy hairs

from him shaving.
          Brut in her nose,

he always threw
          a smile over

his shoulder as he
          walked out the door.

I AIN'T GONNA STAND FOR IT ANYMORE, 1981

When Lee Atwater said,
You start out in 1954
by saying, "Nigger, nigger,
nigger," Denise and Damon
both didn't know nothing
about it, most of America
didn't know either but kind
of did, just as most everybody
in America really know what
the deal is, what our real
history is, what time it is.
Damon likes to end
his sentences with shit
like that and shit like, *You know*
what it is and, *I'm just a Black*
man with the white man
standing on my back. Denise
and Damon didn't need to hear
nobody say nothing about no
Southern strategy to know
the plot, the plot not hidden
but in plain view. Denise saw it
when the rec center closed
again but this time never
reopened, when Lisa stopped
selling her food stamps
because they got cut, when
Denise saw Marcus walking
to work because bus fare
got too high and nobody would
take him, when Miss Angie

started watching folks' children
because Head Start wasn't going
no more, when Uncle Ernie began
taking his pills every other day
because he couldn't afford to take
them every day no more,
when Granny Wilson missed
dialysis four days in a row
and didn't wake up no more.

I CAN MAKE YOU DANCE, 1983

Leaving wasn't as simple

as walking out no door.

It was her house, but she

left just the same, left

just as the sun sets,

as the stretch of horizon

looks more like a sketch

than real life. She left

as snow does, quietly

and with wet tracks.

She left the same way

you leave a town: walk

right out and don't turn

around. With the wind's

breath on her neck, she

left. She left him with his

pipes, with his needles,

with his records, razors,

and that half smile he

used to pry open her

mind when he was lying.

She stepped out of him

and into her. The mirror

appeared familiar, but better.

WEAK AT THE KNEES, 1965

Denise likes Now & Laters,
Pepsi, not Coke, and breakfast,

because nobody can
frown over her

mama's French toast.
She likes to rip

the backside off fireflies
and stick them

to her earlobes
as though they were earrings.

She feels awful
for killing them. The glowing

show she likes though.
She likes her Kool-Aid

blue and her clothes
purple. She thinks folks

just look good
in purple, especially

her with her high yellow
skin. She likes chicken,

but only the skin, and soap
operas because they never

end. If only real life
was like this, she wishes,

because then her granny
would still braid her

hair, and she could still hear
Ella's bright purple knockers

knock as they played
hopscotch in the park.

DAZZ, 1985

Some mornings, without warning,
Damon would wake and declare, *I need*

some air. I need my bare feet on the grass.
I need to be anywhere but here. Here

meaning the city, Mounds State Park
being the anywhere. Even his dreams

have clipped wings, Denise thinks, his
anywhere not able to be something more

than the outer borders of Anderson. Black
folks seldom went to Mounds,

preferring Streaty Park with its netless
basketball hoops and trash-ridden

fences so different than the immaculate
and well-kept trails and grounds

of Mounds. Mounds, where the hills
were burial sites filled with the stone

tools and bones of the Adena people.
Mounds, with its blue, black, white,

and green ash trees' billowing branches
too weak to hold bodies, but wiry

enough for the switches Damon and Denise's
mamas used to make them pick and hit them with, always

weeping afterwards. Denise thought her mother
was so strange, so vain to cry after whooping her backside

until Damon told her about his mama
locking herself in her room all evening

after one of his beatings. Picnicking,
eating red grapes and the bologna sandwiches

Denise makes. Under shaded canopy, the forgiving
grass between their toes, they almost forgot

they better not be caught at this park after dark.

I WISH IT WOULD RAIN, 1977

Same scream since the time before,
the door's closing behind him

at some ungodly hour when the sun ain't
shining, when it ain't night

or day, when nothing but bullets,
booze, and blues can find

their way into your life. Denise
pleads more than yells. The same

scream leaves his lips, the same lies
line his jaw, whet his teeth.

The fire of alcohol on his breath
as he leans in a for kiss: *Baby,*

*I don't know why we argue
like this.* Her scream at this

nonsense is the same scream
as the first time. It will be the same

scream when it's the last time.
Their whole life together,

one wide-mouthed cry sharpening
the dark edges of the night.

GOT TO LOVE SOMEBODY, 1987

A pistol, a razor blade, a crack pipe. A photo
of a woman who loves him more than he
loves liquor and all his other girls. A lighter,
a pint of Thunderbird, a .38 slug, a speaker
to lay his head down by: the bass makes
his face shake. A cigarette, a prayer: *I hope
he's better than me. All I want is for him
to be skinny and better than me, real skinny.*
A crack pipe, a rock, a lighter, a photo,

a prayer: *Help me be better than I am. Help me
to be a man. Make her come back. Make
her come back.* A window, a block, a town:
the factories call his name, crack calls
his name. His eyes are flames. A spark, a rock,
a high that reached out and hugged him
as his mama used to, as Denise used to.
Damon, a man, his record player, his song,
and not a single soul who wants to listen.

MUSTANG SALLY, 1964

Always Denise's daddy was supposed to be
coming: this Sunday at 2:00 p.m., last Saturday

at 4:30, the Friday before that, the Tuesday
before that, as far back as Denise could

remember. As always, there Denise sat
on the crumbling front porch steps. A little

girl among little ruins, the little pink straps
of her backpack securely strapped, waiting

for her father to come back. Between
inspecting big black ants, letting them climb

and scale her hands, she would make believe
each passing car was her father's: that black

Bonneville with the loose and lowered front
bumper looking like a swollen lower lip,

that Pontiac Firebird with the wide, flat hood
that spread out like the table Denise saw white

folks eat at on TV, that Skylark the color of night
after rain clouds sigh and leave the sky,

that dusty old Pinto rusted around the wheel wells.
Denise saw herself in each passenger seat, her daddy

driving, sometimes she had ice cream (Blue Moon
in a cup, not cone—Denise is accident-prone),

sometimes a brown bag full of penny candy. If
her mood was better than fine, then Denise

envisioned Fun Dip with its white dipstick. She
couldn't resist it. The only thing consistent, it's just

Denise and her daddy with nothing but open road
ahead of them and enough time to make up

for every time he left her sitting on that porch until
the streetlights announced it was dinnertime.

TIME WILL REVEAL, 1987

Nobody asked her
what she wanted
for her birthday
so she figured
nobody would do
anything for her
because nobody
even said anything
about her birthday,
so she was so
surprised when she
opened the door
and there he stood,
cake tilted, facing
towards her, her
favorite cousin
Lonnie, Auntie Jessie,
her mama, and silly
Teddy there, too.
Damon counted
to three, and they all
broke out into song.

BIOGRAPHICAL NOTE

Douglas Manuel was born in Anderson, Indiana and now resides in Whittier, California. He received a BA in Creative Writing from Arizona State University, an MFA in poetry from Butler University, and a PhD in English Literature and Creative Writing from the University of Southern California. His first collection of poems, *Testify*, won an IBPA Benjamin Franklin Award for poetry, and his poems and essays can be found in numerous literary journals, magazines, and websites, most recently *Zyzzyva*, *Pleiades*, and the *New Orleans Review*. He has traveled to Egypt and Eritrea with The University of Iowa's International Writing Program to teach poetry. A recipient of the Dana Gioia Poetry Award and a fellowship from the Borchard Foundation Center on Literary Arts, he is a Bayard Rustin Fellow at Whittier College and teaches at Spalding University's low-res MFA program.